JOB'S D...
WOMEN A...

The Madeleva Lecture in Spirituality

This series, sponsored by the Center for Spirituality, Saint Mary's College, Notre Dame, Indiana, honors annually the woman who as president of the college inaugurated its pioneering program in theology, Sister M. Madeleva, C.S.C.

1985
Monika K. Hellwig
Christian Women in a Troubled World

1986
Sandra M. Schneiders
Women and the Word

1987
Mary Collins
Women at Prayer

1988
Maria Harris
Women and Teaching

1989
Elizabeth Dreyer
Passionate Women: Two Medieval Mystics

JOB'S DAUGHTERS: WOMEN AND POWER

JOAN CHITTISTER, O.S.B.

1990 Madeleva Lecture
in Spirituality

PAULIST PRESS
New York/Mahwah

Library of Congress Cataloging-in-Publication Data

Chittister, Joan.
    Job's daughters: women and power/by Joan D. Chittister.
       p. cm.
    "1990 Madeleva lecture in spirituality."
    Includes bibliographical references.
    ISBN 0-8091-3180-3
    1. Woman (Christian theology) 2. Power (Christian theology)
3. Power (Social sciences) 4. Bible. O.T. Job—Criticism, interpretation, etc. I. Title. II. Title: Madeleva lecture in spirituality.
    BT704.C475 1990   90-30517
    261.8′344—dc20   CIP

Published by Paulist Press
997 Macarthur Blvd.
Mahwah, N.J. 07430

Printed and bound in the United States of America

TABLE OF CONTENTS

Sister Joan Chittister is the prioress of the Benedictine Sisters of Erie, Pennsylvania. She is president of the Conference of American Benedictine Prioresses and a past president of the Leadership Conference of Women Religious. She holds a doctorate in social psychology from Penn State University. She is author of *Climb Along the Cutting Edge: An Analysis of Change in Religious Life* (Paulist Press), *Women, Ministry and Church* (Paulist Press), *Winds of Change* (Sheed and Ward), and a forthcoming book, *Distilled from the Daily* (Harper & Row) as well as other books and articles about religious life and contemporary issues.

JOB'S DAUGHTERS: WOMEN AND POWER

"We don't see things as they are; we see them as we are,
Nin wrote."[1] If that's truly the case, there is a lot to be
reconsidered about the nature and place of women,
most of which definitions have not been written by
women but by men who have clearly seen the role of
women from a male point of view.

Aristotle, for instance, wrote once: "Femaleness is
a deformity that affects half the human race."[2] The
position is a harsh one. If femaleness is indeed a deformity, then something is missing in women. If, on the
other hand, femaleness is not a deformity, then something may well be missing in those who think there is. In
fact, whether or not femaleness is more deficiency than
blessing gives basis for the longest standing social and
ecclesiastical debate of all time. What is indisputable,
however, is that, deformity or not, femaleness has indeed been an affliction. The question is to what degree
the affliction is real in our own time and why it is real
and what needs to be done about it if the affliction is to
be removed.

The thesis of this work is that there is operating
among us a false sense of power which holds women in
captivity and the planet in jeopardy. Unless and until

1

both church and state deal with the theology of power that now exists, the social system as we know it will simply continue to deteriorate, with women as its most basic but not its solitary victims.

The classic parable of affliction, the book of Job, traces a history of suffering and a concept of power that may well provide a model for understanding the situation of women in our own day and for dealing with it as well.[3]

There is an element of the book of Job which, I think, warrants special notice. Job, you see, is not a Jew. It is Job, the Gentile, the figure outside the system, who confronts it with the reality of undeserved pain.[4] It is Job, the innocent one, who brings Israel to deal with its own notion of God and life and the theology of sin and suffering. The situation fills a reader with tension. How shall we account for the wanton oppression of whole classes of people—slaves, blacks, women—while others for reasons just as capricious live lives that are self-determined and free of arbitrary controls or groundless suffering. The book of Job confronts us with a dilemma as contemporary as it is overwhelming. Job's suffering is not the plan of God or the will of God or the test of God. It is not God, after all, who is afflicting Job. It is the Accuser who questions Job's endurance and Job's abilities and Job's fidelity.[5] It is the Accuser who sets out to try Job. It is the Accuser who changes Job's life and cuts off Job's opportunities and holds Job in servitude to sorrow. What is to be thought about this? What is to be learned from this by the poor of today's world, by the forgotten of today's world, by the women of today's world?

In Job, too, even the friends of the oppressed blame the victim. It is the reasonable and the orthodox who claim that this suffering is God's will for Job. It is the pious who insist that Job deserves the suffering and will be saved by the suffering and should be glad for the suffering. It is the faithful who insist that Job's plight must have something to do with infidelity. But Job insists on asking why such a thing can be? And Job wants to know the cause of the opprobrium. And Job rails against the suffering and the answers that are being given to it. And Job challenges the world to prove that it is indeed God who has done this thing. And Job wants to know the why of it all. It is Job who says, "I have prepared my defense and I know I am right."[6]

"You are undermining religion and crippling faith in God," Eliphaz the Temanite says. The advice is clear: Don't question your fate. Don't challenge it. Don't resist it. Be docile, in other words. Be obedient, in other words. Accept your proper role in life, in other words.

"We are old. We speak with the wisdom of age," Eliphaz argues. "It's always been this way, in other words. This is clear and constant tradition you are fooling with. This is the custom of time immemorial. "What has made you so wild that you spew your anger at God and spit out such insolent words?"[7]

Sin. Tradition. Wisdom. Obedience. The natural law. God's will. Every argument in the lexicon of the comfortable, the powerful, the pious is used against Job. But Job will not relent. Job demands more than formula faith. Job demands justice. "Enough," Job says. "I have heard enough! I am sick of your consolations. I too could say such things if you were in my position: I could bury you with accusation and sneer at you in my piety or whisper my easy comfort and encourage you with a word."[8] Job's rage has no bounds now. "O earth, do not cover my blood. Never let my cry be buried," he screams.[9] Clearly, there are some things that simply cannot be accepted. There are some things too inhuman for a human being to accept. There are some things that no amount of virtue can absorb without risking the greatest unvirtue of them all, injustice.

Then, not surprisingly, even Job's faith in God begins to waver. Job's love for humanity begins to wither. Job's hope in everything he once thought good begins to pale.

Be obedient, Zophar cautions. Listen to the plan for you.

You are morally inadequate, Eliphaz argues. Realize your condition. God knows I am innocent, Job counters, and God knows that those worse than I reap the graces of the land.[10] "Be humble," the friends insist. "Then God will bless you."[11] Be silent. Be satisfied. Be nothing. And be it all in the name of God.

But Job's strength is stubbornness. Job's power is the unassailability of powerlessness. What else does Job have to lose—except, of course, his integrity, his identity, his self. "I will never let you convict me," he insists. "I will never give up my claim," he promises, though in recognizing his condition and railing against the groundlessness of it all, Job has lost prestige and honor and social place.[12] "Now I am their fool. . . . They stand

4

beside me and sneer. . . . They rush at me in a mob. . . . And now I am in agony," Job laments.[13] To assail the system, Job discovers, is no small task, no reasonable discussion, no simple process. Whatever ideas or creeds or classes the system systematizes are not to be tampered with, not even in the face of the obvious.

Yet to take justice unto himself, to allow his anger to destroy him, to become what he hates, Job learns from God, is no solution either. Job's hope is in God alone. Job's salvation lies in being able to see with new eyes. Job's hope does not rest in avenging the old system but in beginning to envision a new one. Job's transformation lies in being able to distinguish between the designs of God and the destructiveness of evil operating in the name of God. Job's salvation lies in using power well.

Indeed, the cry of Job through history has been a long, long wail.

It has been the wail of Jews on their way to the ovens, struck down by those who claimed the power of God.

It has been the wail of Cambodians in labor camps, struck down by those who claimed the power of God.

It has been the wail of refugees on the West Bank, struck down by those who claimed the power of God.

It has been the wail of dayworkers and the unemployed and the displaced, all struck down by those who claimed the power of God.

It has been the wail of all the forgotten masses of the world.

And today, in our time, Job is a woman.

Job, this voice of universal suffering, fits the fe-

5

male picture all too perfectly: Job was a person faithful to God and compassionate with people. Job had a family and raised them to be true. Job lived responsibly and quietly and piously. Job was gentle and non-violent and trusting. But when Job was afflicted, when Job cried foul, all the weight of the system fell upon his back. Rather than lift the burden from his body, the system condemned Job for his complaint. And Job was told that this senseless degradation was the certain, the conscious, the unending will of God for him.

But, in the last chapter of Job, finally, the sacred writer puts before us one of the most challenging developments in scripture.[14] Those friends and observers of Job's who took upon themselves the task of declaring Job's sufferings to be the will of God for him are humbled. Those who lied about God for the love of God must give tribute, God insists, to the very one they crushed with their unholy use of power. Finally, those orthodox friends of Job's, so smug in their righteousness, so certain in their attitudes, so secure in their superiority, so insistent on the unchangeableness of their brand of orthodoxy, are confronted with the profoundly unorthodox. In Job's world after the scourges are over, when the accusations have ceased and the wrongs have been righted and Job has found that it was not God who was unjust to him and God has found Job to be true, a shocking transformation occurs. Now, in this world where things are finally right, only Job's daughters, not Job's sons, are named—Dove, Cinnamon and Eye-Shadow, the translators call them—and the feminine is allotted an unheard-of equal share of the family inheritance.[15]

In this new world where God's will is no longer thwarted, in other words, those struck down are raised up, the feminine is valued, oppressive power is disempowered so that the powerless can triumph, the relationships of the world are reordered and hope is made new in Job's daughters. In this new vision Job sets the feminine free. Job uses his power to eliminate the divisions that put people in contention. Job uses his power to make his world whole.

Indeed, Job is a story of power gone awry: the Accuser, the friends, the society all claim that Job is Job's problem, that Job is inherently inadequate and deserving of his state, that in Job's nature itself lies the fault of his own suffering, that Job is deficient, morally deformed, spiritually inadequate, that Job deserves what Job is getting, that God has ordained it so and that salvation for Job depends on humble acquiescence.

Job's story is, indeed, the story of any woman in the world today who suffers the arbitrary judgment of femaleness, who bears oppression in her own body, who is faithful to God and is told that God is the reason for her suffering, who has known what it is to have people blame the victim, who asks questions and is called heretic for the asking, and whose future is in her daughters as well as in her sons.

Job's friends use ideology, office and law against him, too. They blame the victim, they remind him of his status in life, they claim that his suffering is due him, they insist that all the degradation is the will of God for him. Women recognize all the theory.

Women, too, have been taught that if they are raped and beaten it is their own fault. They have been

7

taught that they are intellectually, emotionally and morally inferior to men. They have been taught that suffering is their lot in life. They have been taught that God favors men but not women. They have been taught that God is male and that, therefore, males are closer to God.

They have been taught, like Job, to accept their lot without question. They have been taught that questions are heretical.

They have learned best what the theorists have only speculated about: power indeed profits the powerful. Those who occupy society's positions and interpret its ideologies and write its laws have power. Those who do not, do not. Women have been taught to believe that things as they are, are things that are good for them so that they will endorse their own oppression and maintain the powerful in power unimpeded.

And, like Job, they are questioning, contending, rebelling. Everywhere.

The question for our time is: What does the story of Job and Job's daughters have to say about the condition of women in the world today? Most of all, what does it say about our own present use of power. What does it say about hope for the future?

To deal with these questions, it is necessary to consider five elements: (1) the nature of power; (2) the relationship of women's circumstances to the nature of power; (3) the question of female deformity and power; (4) the feminist agenda in the world today and the powers that affect it; (5) the challenge of Job's daughters to the twenty-first century.

Power, as Job was quick to discover, is a very complex concept. It is not always found where it may be expected to be. It does not always work to the world's advantage. It is not easily controlled. It is not always official.

"Power," Max Weber wrote, "is the probability that one actor within a social relationship will be in a position to carry out [their] will despite resistance, regardless of the basis on which this probability rests."[16]

Power, in other words, is the ability to implement decisions, to make things happen. People with power don't hope that someone will listen to them, they know that someone will listen to them. Power does not expect favors; power expects results. Power has status or resources or both. Power is not dependent.

Power can also be lost as well as achieved. In fact, power based on overt force is the most tenuous power of all since it is the most vulnerable to contest. People do not take oppression lightly. People resist it even when they cannot overthrow it. People withhold their love from their oppressors and they withhold their approval and they withhold themselves. Relationships that are maintained only by force are not really relationships at all. They are simply arrangements that last only until the oppression can be removed.

Effective power, long-term power, on the other hand, depends for its energy, Weber argues, on three factors: the opportunity to make the rules, the right to sanction those who break them, and the means to control thought and transmit ideas. People who tell us what we should do and how we should do it and why it must be done are really people with power.

The right to determine who shall be slave and who shall be free in a country, who shall vote and who shall not, who may work and who may not is the power it takes to control the entire society. The right to punish those slaves who drink at the water fountains of whites or to jail those women who participate in sit-ins at polling booths is the power to keep other women from even attempting to vote. The capacity to control the media or the synods or the schools that write the arguments or publish the ecclesiastical documents or create the textbooks is the power to form the attitudes and shape the cultural constructs of a society in such a way that a people come to believe that what is done to them is right for them and good for them and immutable for them.

This power, Weber argues, to redefine the interests of the public so that they believe that their interests coincide with those of the leaders and to motivate followers to voluntary obedience to rules is the greatest power of them all. Here opposition ceases and the oppressed internalize the message of the oppressor until it doesn't take force to keep the powerless from seeking power. All it takes is the continuation of the idea.

It is not necessary to believe that this kind of consolidation of power represents a conspiracy to oppress. Oppression is a serious enough affliction without adding paranoia to it. William Graham Sumner's highly respected thesis, on the contrary, posits that social norms and values are the result of long and essentially unconscious social development.[17] It is important nevertheless, to recognize that the social norms that develop through time stand, almost inevitably, to benefit the powerful who see the world from where they stand, rather than the poor, the uneducated or the powerless who have little place in that society and have been forgotten by it.[18]

The point being made most commonly by conflict theorists, obviously, is that power is not necessarily a given. It is gained, consolidated and maintained through clearly observable means. It concentrates in specific places to the advantage of certain people. What is even more important to us at this moment in history, however, is the idea that power is not of a single piece. All uses of power do not look the same and are not used in the same ways.

The psychiatrist Rollo May, in fact, defines five kinds of power: exploitative power, competitive power, manipulative power, nurturant power and integrative power.[19] Each of the models, according to May, has a different end. Each of them comes out of a different world view. Each of them has a different center. But each of them is intent on control. And in each of these dimensions of influence and control lies the sad and enduring history of women. In each of them, as well, lies choices for and against a holy future. It is one thing to talk about democracy and collegiality, about equality and the priesthood of all the believers, about universal political participation and charism, about opportunity and grace. It is another thing entirely to develop the

11

kind of theology of power that will honestly enable the accomplishment of these concepts.

Exploitative Power. According to May's paradigm, exploitative power is power that uses the other for the service of the self. Exploitative power is power *over* another. Slave owners exploit slaves, sometimes kindly, true, but always for the sake of the owner, never for the sake of the slave.

The purpose of exploitative power—either brutal or benign—is to drain the other of whatever power the exploited might lay claim to in order to advance the purposes of the rulers themselves. To take property and civil rights and human dignity away from Jews in Germany is to wield exploitative power. To send American blacks, in disproportionate numbers, onto the front lines in Europe when they could not vote in their own home towns in the United States was pure exploitation. Exploitation justifies itself on the basis of a greater good. The exploiter does what is "good" for people who are not allowed to do what is good for themselves.

The structure best suited to exploitative power, of course, is hierarchy. In this system one person or group of people is clearly in charge. Everybody else is simply a minion of the system.

Exploitation directs people, it does not respond to them. Even the questions themselves, in fact, are seen as instances of treasonous infidelity or arrogant rebellion in a world where exploitation is the climate and character of the ruling class.

Exploitation rests on very clear assumptions about rights and roles and the purpose of authority. Exploitative power assumes that people, too, are simply resources to be consumed, interchangeable parts designed to maintain the leader and the organization and the system, rather than to grow and prosper in their own right. Exploitative power assumes that some people are destined to be in charge, that some people are born to rule, that some people are divinely designated to stand in the place of God with the fullness of God for the sake of God. Exploitative power assumes that truth and right and prerogative are in the hands of some, but not all, and that by nature. Exploitative power, in other words, rests upon the notion that some people have the right to control other people.

The theology of exploitation is a seductive one. It is based on the notion that some people are endowed with clearer vision and closer association to the divine. Those who are superior to other people know their superiority, claim it as essential and natural, and claim for their cause the quality of the common good. Hitler was ridding the world of inferiors so that the superior race could flourish. Industrialists exploited workers so that through the efforts of the expendable lower classes, business would develop. Communism, the ideal state, rode to power on the backs of defeated masses of ethnic groups considered essential to the security of the state. Children were sacrificed by adults to sweatshops because they were simply children and unable to defend their own interests and were expendable.

Everywhere, exploitation rides on the same claims: there is something—some work, some state, some creed, some doctrine—more important than the people who are crushed under its weight.

Job is exploited by the Accuser so that truth would be known and fidelity tested.

Women and Exploitative Power. Of all the groups in history affected by exploitative power, women hold un-contested first place. The oldest hieroglyphic symbol for "slave" is "woman held in hand." In Herman Nie-boer's definitive work on slavery, *Slavery as an Industrial System,* published in 1900, women were not included in the study despite the fact that historians agree women were the world's first slaves.[20] Nieboer's explanation for the omission of women's stories in a social system that was made up almost entirely of women was a chill-ing one: "Slavery proper," he writes, "does not exist where there are none but female slaves."[21] The subjec-tion of women, in other words, is natural, an essential part of the female condition, widespread and to be taken for granted. Women are born to be slaves. It is their role in life. It is God's will for them.

The idea had honored support. Plato, who philoso-phers maintain was actually ahead of his time on the subject of women, was nonetheless clear in his classifi-cation of them as basically inferior or secondary to men. He wrote in *The Timaeus*[22] that women were cre-ated from wicked men as a punishment for their having been irrational. He argued in *Laws,*[23] *The Letters*[24] and *Theaetetus*[25] that women were essentially and naturally inferior and were to be categorized with children and animals.

Aristotle declared women naturally inferior three hundred years before the birth of Christ.[26] Thomas Aquinas dignified that position in Catholic theology in the thirteenth century with the conclusion that given the fact that they were "subordinate both in purpose (sex) and material (size)," they were therefore affected negatively "both in reason and in moral discernment."[27]

The finest thinkers of the centuries, in other words, set the ideological stage for the forcible oppression of women. As a result, Matthew Bacon could still argue in the seventeenth century that by law a husband has "power and dominion over his wife to keep her by force within the bounds of duty."[28] And the British barrister Blackstone could still be affirmed in the courts of the nineteenth century in his argument that "a husband is responsible for his wife's behavior."[29]

Finally, laws governing women became models for the slavery legislation of the United States. The controlling ideology of male supremacy made the worst of things possible. Women were bought and sold, raped and beaten, captured and kept, used and thrown away with impunity and throughout the world.

Even the ceremony marking the sacrament of marriage itself symbolized all too clearly the essentially subservient state of even the most capable, and most loved, of women: women took the vow to obey, not the man; women lost their very identities to become his other self; women were marked with a ring; women were veiled as a sign of their withdrawal from public life; women were "given away" from one man to another. Finally, the pair itself were pronounced "man and wife," not husband and wife, or man and woman, but man and thing, man and the domestic servant he had acquired. It was the Greek statesman Demosthenes who said it most forthrightly, perhaps: "We have," he argued, "*hetairae* for our delight, concubines for the daily needs of our bodies, wives in order that we may beget legitimate children and have faithful house-keepers."[30]

Clearly, it is only a short distance from that type of science and that kind of philosophy and that brand of theology and that manner of lawmaking to the exploitation of women in every arena. And who would speak out against it? Indeed, who was there to speak out when women themselves had been kept out of the very systems that could have enabled them to speak out—out of education and out of politics and out of the economic system? Most of all, who benefited from it?

The exploitation of women, in fact, had become so commonplace that it was not even noticed by men, not even questioned by women. So natural, so normal was the phenomenon of female degradation that the whole world, women and men alike, called it "woman's role."

The consolidation of power was complete. It was a Weberian classic: men made the rules that governed the relationship between the sexes; men administered the sanctions which maintained them; and men were the idea-agents and spokespersons who communicated their meaning, infused them with moral value and persuaded both men and women that the arrangements were in the best interests of women themselves.

It is a pure demonstration of exploitative power to pay women less than we pay men for the very same teaching and the very same administration and the very same cooking in both cheap and high class restaurants, but we have been taught that men are the providers of the family, not women. So, despite the fact that two-thirds of the single parent homes of the world are headed by women, we persist in that thinking and maintain those laws and starve women and children everywhere.

It is a blatant use of exploitative power to make the raising of children the major responsibility of women, but someone has defined mothering instead of father-ing as the primary familial responsibility and mothering rather than parenting as the nature of childrearing and called it woman's role.

It is an obvious use of exploitative power to arrest prostitutes but not johns, but we have made sexuality, too, the responsibility of women alone and for cen-turies blamed women for what men apparently cannot not do.

Exploitative power is power used against another for personal gain. Women have been used, as a matter of course, for the enrichment, convenience and profit of others.

Competitive Power. In May's schema, competitive power is power used for conquest. Competitive power is power directed against others in order to defeat them. The purpose of competition, in other words, is as much to put another down as it is to build the self up.

The problem with competition is twofold. First, it always sets out to control the field, to eliminate, to supersede. Worse, perhaps, it makes human value de-pend on the devaluation of others. It implies, at least indirectly, that a person is only as good as that person

17

can make others look inferior. "Nobody remembers who comes in second," the aphorism reminds us. Being first, in other words, is the only position worth having in life.

Children learn at a very early age, consequently, that it is better not to try than it is to fail. In a competitive society, people grow up unaware of the sheer joy of playing games. Competitive people play only to win them. What others do is fuel for personal achievement rather than for communal pride. What others can do, I must do better. In such a culture, individualism reigns supreme and community dies on the vine.

It is competitive power that insists that the United States of America be number one in an arms race that is already over-deadly. It is competitive power that deals in scores and numbers and evaluations. It is competitive power that defines enemies.

The structure basic to competition is the team mentality. We identify the people on our side, the ones intent on claiming all advantage for ourselves, and then we pour our energies into maintaining our lead, or retaining our positions, or outgaining the field. There is little room in competition for a genuine respect for the other. The human gifts of others are to be disparaged, not developed. When competition is the basis of my drive for power, it is my team, my clan, my state, my company, my church, my role that pre-empts every other consideration.

A competitive world rests on the notion of losers. Defeat is built into the fabric of life. In every political situation, in every business venture, in every organization, people are silently measured for relative strength, relative intelligence, relative skill, relative value and relative challenge. Worse, everyone is a potential threat. As a result, no one is really welcomed into the field or into the arena or into the society. Personal security is always at a premium because in a world where competition reigns, we never know who may unseat us. It is best to keep a distance. It is better to rule in grand isolation than to risk not ruling at all.

In a competitive society, obviously, no matter what the rhetoric of equality may be, power is not meant to be shared. On the contrary, to survive, power must be constantly tested and constantly gained, whatever the cost. In competing with the Soviet Union for military supremacy, we have lost the value of that nation's ideals and bartered our own claims to concern for human development in exchange for the egotistic distinction of being the one nation most able to destroy the world. In competing for markets around the world, we have lost sight of the effect of our economic policies on the economies of other countries. In competing for wealth, we have impoverished others.

Competitive power is based on the assumption that in order to win someone must lose. A competitive society assumes that some people are by nature better than others and must be able to prove it. In a competitive world people expect that building themselves up depends on their being able to put someone else down.

Where exploitative power depends on the use of force to achieve the good of the masters, competitive power is intent on proving the right to exclusive control.

The theology of competitive power is a simple one:

some people, by dint of special effort and special gifts, have the God-given right to rule. Special abilities require special consideration. Special gifts cannot be denied. And once the winner of the contest has been declared, no one dare question the criteria of judgment or the quality of the work or the specialness of the endowment. What people compete for and win is forever theirs, especially if they are smart enough to close the competition. The United States and Russia, for instance, have barred the development of nuclear weapons to other countries. Other countries, the thinking goes, are not moral enough, or capable enough, or sane enough, to be permitted the same nuclear opportunities as the superpowers, who it is assumed are supremely endowed to hold the life of the rest of the world in their controlling hands. Everything Japanese that was once an uncontested U.S. product is now labeled as dishonest filching of U.S. technology rather than a superior application of common knowledge.

Competition, it is clear, pits people against one another: the young against the old, the employee against the employer, men against women, race against race. Where competition is the prevailing climate, people lose sight of the whole and the world is broken up into contending factions instead of welded into one great mutually reinforcing community of people with the same gifts and the same goals.

When competitive power infects personal relationships, the struggle is always to prove the right of place. Every position in every department is geared to reward standard performances of achievement rather than to encourage creativity. Parents bait their own children against one another. Churches decide who is more acceptable to God than others on the basis of rules of which God, it is likely, has never heard.

Competitive power engages the energies of a people into keeping other people out instead of drawing other people into our lives and our structures and our institutions. The nation says that competition is what makes us economically successful and the church says that competition is what gets us higher places in a heaven that is geared only to winners.

The theology of competition is a theology of perfectionism based on individual performance that destroys precisely what it sets out to enable, the development of all.

Women and Competitive Power. Men as a class, Plato taught in the *Republic,* are naturally superior to women. "There is nothing that women (as a class) can do better than men (as a class) . . . even in spheres reserved to women," he wrote.[31] The question becomes then: What really is the "role of women"? Do women, in fact, have any real "role" at all? The history of women from early societies to our own seems to negate the idea.

Male competition with women has been very subtle. The way not to lose to a woman is to deny her the right to play the game at all. With the ideology of natural inferiority and moral incapacity firmly entrenched, it was only logical to deny education to women. "Girls need only sufficient geography to find their way around the house and enough chemistry to keep the pot boiling," it was said. The Supreme Court ruled in 1872, in fact, that "the timidity and delicacy of the female sex

21

unfits it for many occupations in civil life."[32] Schools, therefore, accepted girls only in the summertime when boys had left the classrooms for the fields. The curriculum of course, was a diluted one designed only to enable a woman to be the wifely assistant to a man: writing, drawing, embroidery, music, dancing and religious readings.

No independent secular college accepted women until Oberlin in Ohio opened its doors to women in 1850, and then only provided that they were willing to do the wash, clean the rooms and serve the meals of the male students.[33] In 1896, Notre Dame of Maryland was opened for women students, but no male Catholic college would accept women until 1911, when Catholic University of America finally allowed women to take courses, provided that the classes were held off-campus.[34]

In 1970, women were still being admitted to major colleges on quota systems. The reason women were not artists and musicians and doctors and lawyers is clear. They simply could not get the education or the support that it took to do such things.

Consequently, even in our own time, women are more likely to be waitresses than chefs, stewardesses than pilots, nurses than doctors, stenographers than lawyers. It is not that they have lost to the competition. The fact is that they have not even been allowed to compete.

So-called "protective labor legislation" barred employment to women in any jobs that called for the worker to lift more than thirty pounds. These laws, enacted for the good of women, of course, kept women who commonly carried three-year olds and wet wash and market baskets for miles out of jobs and out of unions that could have gained them economic independence and the self-direction that self-sufficiency brings.

The teamwork of competitive power simply kept women off the team, out of the courts, away from the idea-formation arena of the world of higher academics, out of the theology journals, distant from one another and the world around them, out of touch and out of contact with any system, ecclesiastical or civil, that legislated for them with no reference to them at all.

Rape, the ultimate conquest, which even now occurs in the United States alone every six minutes, the government tells us, became a way of life.[35] Women were booty and women were objects. Women were not full persons in their own right.

Male clubs and male golf courses and male games and male occupations—the whole male world was closed to women. Their place was in the home, it was said, and they were kept there, out of sight and out of competition with men.

Women became invisible. Men, as the Haitians say, took up all the space.

Manipulative Power. Personal aggrandizement is not always achieved by either force or structural suppression. There is a kind of power that is far more artful than that. Where exploitation uses others for personal gain and competition works against others to defeat them, manipulative power uses indirect control to manage them.

23

Manipulation distorts events or ideas in such a way that they cannot possibly be seen clearly and objectively. Manipulators provide information, for instance, but only part of it. They always look as if they are open to new ideas or people but manipulators distort the flow of information or events in such a way that they confirm the worst fears of the group about the unknown. When data is manipulated we see only the worst—or the best—parts of it. We see, in other words, only what the manipulator wants us to see. We hear only what the manipulator wants us to hear. We experience only what the manipulator wants us to experience.

When manipulation is the technique used to retain power, society sees only one side of the world. The other side is presented in distorted or defamed or destructive ways that make it essential to leave power in the hands of the powerful in order to save us from what we have already rejected without cause.

But if a people can be made to demand what is bad for them, the power of the powerful is all the more potent. Then power becomes legitimate rather than illegitimate. Then power is gained because it has been given rather than having to be taken by force. Then ideology smooths the way for the otherwise unthinkable.

Karl Marx, for instance, dealt almost exclusively with the illegitimate use of power. Marx emphasized the fact that people can control the behaviors of others by depriving them of economic independence, or by using force or by keeping them in ignorance.[36] Max Weber, on the other hand, dealt in great detail with the processes by which power is legitimated in a society.[37] The means of achieving legitimate power, it seems, were a great deal more interesting to Weber than the study of illegitimate power and for good reason. To say that power is legitimate is to recognize that the power wielded over the powerless of a society is accepted by the powerless themselves. Then the possibility of revolution is remote. Then the powerful have total security and the powerless are left only with the assurance that they will get for themselves what they themselves think that they deserve.

Marx's theory assumes the revolution of the masses to redress their grievances. Marx was sure that when people discovered that they were being used for the advantage of an upper class or suppressed to maintain an upper class they would rise up to right the imbalance. Weber, on the other hand, knew better. Weber assumed that people will accept whatever they have been taught to believe is the proper order of things, the will of God for them, the natural law, their lot in life. Weber recognized that it was more important for the powerful to control the ideas of a people than to control their bodies. It was slaves, after all, who doubted their own ability to live away from the plantations where "the massa" provided what they were unable to achieve for themselves. It is far too often women themselves who wonder whether or not a woman is really strong enough to be president.

Weber defines the three ways that power is legitimated: by law, by tradition and by custom. When office, ideology or practice confirms the authority of a leader or a group, in other words, the powerless themselves will begin to enforce conformity to it by social sanctions or rewards. Since the community supports the powerful, therefore, the onus for non-conformity will fall upon the follower who resists the system. The black, for instance, who stepped out of line was just as often chided by blacks as by whites. The woman who worked out of the home was as commonly criticized by other women as by men. So adroitly had the ideology been constructed, in other words, that men did not have to worry about correcting dangerous departures from it. Women themselves corrected other women for trying to break out of the mold.

The point is obvious: if the president commands something, or past teaching requires something, or historical practice dictates something, then departure from the norm is not only difficult, it is often even resisted by the very people who would stand to profit most from change. The most important thing that the powerful must do then, Weber points out, is to motivate others to accept the system they represent and to accede to its internal authority.

Since the legitimacy of power rests in the minds of the masses, not in the inherency of the powerful, manipulation is key to being able to maintain a system where people are made to be less than they can be.

Ideology and tokenism and propaganda, consequently, are the keystones of manipulation.

Ideology, of course, is the ideals and images and beliefs which are taught in the schools, formed in the homes and enshrined in the laws of a people and upon which the society bases its structures and behaviors. To teach that God is male is an ideology. To promote the idea that women are psychologically inferior is an ideology. To heap up a philosophy and theology and sociology that assumes that women are second-class, derivative, "deformed" human beings is to build a superstructure of thought that filters out the true dimensions of life. The world has been faced with the ideology of the super race and rejected it. The world has dealt with the ideology of fascism and rejected it. The world has suffered under the ideology of dualism and renounced it. To be whole, the world will have to unmask the ideology of female inequality as well or we will continue to look upon the world with a one-eyed view.

Tokenism is the practice of unproportionate representation of the powerless. Tokenism co-opts outsiders into the power structure in small numbers in order to look accepting of the total group but without really having to share power with them. One black on the board of the local bank can hardly change the investment policies of the entire system. One lay person on the bishop's advisory council looks good but does not change the clerical nature of diocesan decision-making. One handicapped employee in the plant does not make it an equal-opportunity employer. But they do make the bank and the council and the plant look open to blacks and lay people and the handicapped. Tokenism takes a few outsiders into the center of a system in order to keep the rest of the group standing quietly on the edges.

Tokenism manipulates reality by making it look like something it isn't. It sets out to disguise an oppressive reality. It baits people with the promise of possibility which, by its very nature, it is intent on denying. Tokenism includes a few to claim fairness but is by that very process able to avoid equality.

Propaganda, on the other hand, is a more blatant form of manipulation than tokenism but no less difficult to unmask. Propaganda manipulates by presenting only part of a reality. By refusing to examine an issue from every perspective, propaganda can block the ability to evaluate the negative effects of law or ideology or custom. The suppression of the full history of Joseph Stalin in the Soviet Union, for instance, has retarded the political development of that nation drastically. The fact that Americans were never told that Japan had already sued for peace before the dropping of the atomic bomb and never saw the effects of the bombing until years after the fact has helped to buttress the idea of messianic Americanism and fuel the deterrence argument in the United States for over four decades.

Worse than the fact that propaganda presents only one side of an issue, however, is the fact that it often sets out deliberately to present only one dimension of an issue or to distort a single facet of it. The ideals of communism have never been officially presented in the United States in a positive fashion. Only "the communist threat" has been emphasized. Americans have yet to hear about the smoldering anger Mexicans still harbor against the United States over the American invasion of Mexican territory and their subsequent loss of Texas and Colorado, the potentially richest region of that country, to the United States. We have, however, been given a very clear picture of roaming banditos and the Alamo and the wetbacks who are coming to the United States illegally to steal U.S. jobs.

Propaganda makes sure that people see what people with the resources to shape the images want them to see. Propagandists make all Germans Huns and all communists evil and all American warfare pure.

Propaganda forms ideas and propaganda forms minds. And so, propaganda shapes law and society as well.

The point is that both tokenism and propaganda have a great deal to do with keeping people down and keeping truth hidden even while they look like they are doing precisely the opposite: taking people in and getting the truth out.

Women and Manipulative Power. Tokenism and propaganda have been used in almost symphonic proportions in the life history of women.

Particularly since the advent of the modern woman's movement, tokenism has been raised to high art. There are a few women everywhere: a few women in Congress, a few women on road gangs, a few women in the Vatican, a few women in the front office. Nowhere, however, do women balance in number the volume of women in the system or the volume of men who control those areas.

There have always, in fact, been a few women in every area whom men have held up as proof of their unprejudiced acceptance of women. There have been a few women saints—all carefully chosen by men, of course—and there have been a few women leaders and a few women entrepreneurs, most of them more the beneficiaries of inheritance laws than the products of non-sexist societies. Or, as Gibbon puts it in *The Decline and Fall of the Roman Empire,* women leaders in history are "a singular exception . . . a woman is often acknowledged the absolute sovereign of a great kingdom, in which she would be deemed incapable of exercising the smallest employment, civil or military."[38]

The explanations that history serves up for the phenomenon of competent women in roles normally reserved to men include the notion that women in power have either had strong men to direct them—as if men in power are not also directed by strong subordinates—or that there was always something a bit unfeminine about them, or that their very feminine weakness disposed them to negotiate where men would have fought and won.

The problem is that what is seen as an exception is not a freedom won; it is seen as a favor given or a mistake survived. Singular tokens do not satisfy for the lost human aspirations of an entire class of human beings. All that tokens do is to prove that their kind are capable of doing what is needed to be done. Tokens do not open the doors of opportunity to an entire class; tokens simply mask the fact, in a dishonest and deleterious way, that the doors are not really open at all.

Propaganda is the archpiece in the manipulative treatment of women.

Women, their male definers have taught, are more emotional, less stable, more frail, less intelligent, more illogical, less capable of stress than men. On these grounds women have been kept out of public service and kept from self-direction as well. The truth is that if everything that men have said about women is true, then women aren't fit to be mothers.

Modern social science research, however, simply does not support those conclusions. Furthermore, the publication of these results in popular journals is beginning to offset the effects of centuries of negative propaganda about women's roles, nature and personalities.

The Maccoby studies, for instance, have confirmed the fact that women students are as bright as male students up to the first year of college but that by then women who have been trained to believe that intellectualism is unfeminine or that men reject women who are brighter than themselves begin to fear success and to fall behind in school.[39] Achievement motivation, consequently, is more complex in women than in men for whom success is part of their social definition. It isn't ladylike to be intellectual, girls learn. "A man is, in general, better pleased," Samuel Johnson wrote, "when he has a good dinner upon his table, than when his wife talks Greek." Women bear the brunt of that dictum yet.

According to the endocrinologist Estelle Ramey, the aging process that leads to earlier death in men than in women is a factor of the male hormone.[40] But if that is the case, it is not anatomy that is destiny, as Freud argued; it is the cortex that determines our longevity and our long-term endurance. The notion that women are weaker than men is thus a very one-dimensional argument.

Social scientists Johnson and Goodchild report that the feminine strategies women have used to get their way in the absence of real power—helplessness, tears and ingratiation—actually diminish the amount of human respect they are accorded and, in addition, damage their own self-esteem.[41] Neither women nor men, in other words, really like a simpering, finagling woman. Yet men reject women who are direct or expert as well. The double bind that this imposes on women is clearly designed to leave them both helpless and mute.

Finally, research models like the Maccoby-Jacklin studies[42] report that girls are no more social than boys, no more concerned with people than boys are and no more dependent on caretakers. At the same time, the study shows, boys are no more willing than girls to stay alone. The researchers found, too, that girls are no more suggestible than boys and that, in fact, boys and girls are both equally susceptible to persuasive communications. Neither sex, it seems, is more naturally "logical" or more uncontrollably gullible than the other.

At the same time, the social scientists do find that males are more aggressive than females and that though girls are just as motivated to achieve as boys, the findings indicate that girls are not motivated, as boys are, to compete.

Girls, the studies show repeatedly, have greater verbal ability than boys and by age eleven have become superior to boys in understanding and language production. At the same time, boys excel in visual-spatial ability and perceive the relationship of objects in space with more facility than girls do. The most important finding of the study, however, may be that the sexes are equal in general analytical ability. The skills, it seems, are complementary, not exclusive. Both are highly valuable and either without the other is limited.

Most damaging of all, perhaps, has been the effect of religious ideology on the status of women. The image of Eve as the seducer of man and the sinner who lost paradise for the human race, despite Adam's equal responsibility, moral intelligence and awareness, has been used for centuries to justify the exclusion of women from male enclaves and holy places.

The use of biblical images of the creation of women from the rib of a man to assert the subservience of women rather than their equality as "bone of my bone, flesh of my flesh," has relegated women to second-class status throughout modern history.

The notion that the male is more the image of God than the female despite the fact that Genesis says exactly the opposite has been used to prove the basic superiority of man. The male's relative nearness to the divine man has made maleness normative. It has reduced the value of the incarnation from the human to the male. It has made the residual suspicion of the spiritual nature of women rampant.

Even the translations of the scriptures have been used to reinforce the notion of the secondary role of women. Official publications of the Bible, for instance, choose to translate the Hebrew words *ezer* and *kenegdo* in Genesis as "helper" and "fit" rather than "strength" and "equal," as they are in other places in the same work, so that the phrase is made to read that woman is "a helper fit for man," rather than what linguists say is an equally acceptable alternate rendering that woman is "a power equal to man."[43]

The implications are obvious. We have etched women in the human mind as lesser, undeveloped, basically incompetent, inept and needful of direction and control. What is worse, the ideas have not been engrained simply by virtue of the fact that we never said the opposite. The ideas have actually been taught.

In a work on the *Sacrament of Orders*, published in 1962 by Emmanuel D'Lorenzo, O.M.I., then on the theology faculty of the Catholic University of America, D'Lorenzo teaches that "the reason . . . for denying women the right to teach is a reason that is absolute and universal, based as it is on the natural condition of inferiority and subjection that is the portion of women. . . . This moral feebleness," the text goes on to explain, "is manifest at once in lightness of judgment, in credulity . . . and finally in the fragility of spirit by which she is less able to rein in the passions, particularly concupiscence."[44]

Obviously, the propaganda against women has been extremely successful. Most men and many women themselves have accepted the fact that women are by nature deficient. The result, of course, is that the human race has been systematically deprived of the best part of at least half of its human resources. The more obvious result, however, is the fact that the other half of the human race has managed to hold power without contest and even at the request of the women who have

34

been limited in their development by the ideology of female deformity.

The point is clear: By labeling women negatively, by defining them only in prejudicial terms, by treating their achievements as exceptions rather than as normative, women's place in both church and society has been controlled by propaganda and tokenism.

The book of Job is replete with instances of exploitation and moral competition and theological manipulation. The Accuser harasses Job to maintain his own role as arbiter of goodness and prove his own superiority.[45] Job's friend, Eliphaz, simply urges Job to admit his weakness and to try harder, as if what Job already was, was not enough.[46] Bildad[47] and Zophar[48] paint God as the hounder of sinners and refuse to see beyond the theological premise of the times which taught that misfortune was the result of sin and that people, therefore, bring misfortune down upon their own heads.

Indeed, power can take the best of people and destroy them. If exploitative and competitive and manipulative power are the coin of the realm, it is not necessarily true that good will win out and righteousness will triumph and the meek will prevail.

But Rollo May, like Marx and Weber, recognizes, too, that there are types of power that develop rather than destroy. Nurturing power and integrative power, May says, are power used to bring all life to fullness.

Nurturant Power. Nurturant power is power that works for the sake of the other. The purpose of nurturant power is to develop and enable the other so that the members of the human community can be strengthened by one another's gifts. Growth and autonomy become the foundations of any group that embraces the ideals of nurturant power. The goal of the nurturant leader is not to make people dependent. It is to make people capable of acting independently and to the best of their abilities so that the whole group can be stronger as a result.

Whereas groups that practice oppression or coercion will eventually invite either disaffection or rebellion, the society that nurtures people to fullness of life is a society that multiplies its resources and confirms its right to exist.

What a group nurtures, it will reap. Dependency, rigidity, subservience, conformity and self-hatred all stamp out creativity and dynamism. Children who have not been prepared for adulthood by careful independence training are children who become the neurotics of the next generation. Either they cling to past patterns that have long since become counter-productive or they live in fear of the next challenge for which they have developed no confidence to confront. They become eternal children.

Groups that foster coercion and control and conformity rather than growth and autonomy stagnate quickly until even the powerful of that society are disappointed with what they have created. The reorganization of Soviet society is not necessary because the old system failed. *Perestroika* is necessary precisely because the old system succeeded so well. The communist state set out to create a faceless, mindless, one-dimensional society and it worked. People learned to feel little responsibility, show little initiative and take only limited responsibility for the development of the nation. But now that the individual giftedness has been stamped out, the state itself is awash in its own powerlessness.

The history of race relations and immigration in the United States where competition is central to the very working of the system itself is every bit as revealing. People we have made an underclass without opportunity and hope we call shiftless. Whom we refuse to employ we call lazy. Whom we have kept illiterate, we call ignorant.

Nurturant power, on the other hand, is power that educates and parents and advocates for the sake of the other. The basic structure of the nurturant society is community. In the nurturant society there is clear understanding that the gifts of one of us enhance the lives of all of us. If the poor were not poor, our cities would be more beautiful. If the disadvantaged were not disadvantaged our future as a nation would be clearer. If the uneducated were not uneducated our highly technological society could be more confident in the face of foreign competition and our job markets more secure. With a sense of community, pathological individualism would disappear.

Nurturant power is based on the assumption that if people are enabled to develop, their development will benefit us all. It assumes, furthermore, that all people are born with gifts the rest of the people need. It assumes, finally, that none of us are meant to be the footstools of the rest of us.

Those assumptions, of course, fly in the face of a

Darwinian world intent on self-aggrandizement and wedded to theories of social evolution despite realities to the contrary. The idea that development from lower to higher forms of social organization or from simple to complex forms of relationship automatically leads to a better state of life where the ineffective and the inadequate are eventually cast off forever is historically untrue. Technology did not bring progress in all aspects of life. Industrialization did not right social imbalances. World War I was not "the war to end all wars." The white race has not been more moral, more effective or more successful than races and civilizations before it.

The point of creation-centered theology is that some of us are not higher species than the rest of us. No type or class of people has the right to assume that they are inherently better than the rest of the people since all of humanity springs from one source. On the contrary, nurturing power is based on the theology of creation, the notion that all things are created good and that all things bear within them a spark of the divine. But if that is true, then to name anyone a lesser image of God is to demean the very idea of God the creator because it implies that some sparks of the divine in the human soul are better, fuller, more authentic sparks than others.

Nurturing power, consequently, is not devoted to building one group up by bringing another group down. Nurturing power is intent on releasing the energies and gifts in all of us so that we can all rise up together, so that all of us have access to all the abilities available to the rest of us. Nurturant power does not stereotype or limit or categorize people according to race or class or gender. Nurturant power builds the self by building the other.

When Job begins to accept life without having to have reasons for everything, when Job simply begins to take life on its own terms without having to blame God for it, when Job is free to live life as life is meant to be lived by seeing the good in the worst of it, when Job is able to nurture what he has rather than to need to control it or eliminate it, Job begins to see his daughters as well as his sons and his whole world changes, his blessings are multiplied and his world begins to flourish.[49]

Women and Nurturant Power. The question is not whether or not women nurture. Nurturance is indeed the only role comfortably awarded to women and that for the sake of the men who control them. The question is whether or not women's gifts are nurtured as well. The answers are in the statistics. If indeed the researchers are right and the intellectual capacities and the moral qualities and the emotional needs of women are the same as those of men, then we should surely see women developing those abilities in many of the same ways and fields that men do. The fact is, however, that very little other than motherhood and homemaking have been open to women to satisfy their own needs to create and build and enjoy. Even now with the advent of the women's movement, the field is a great deal more limited than imagination would have it.

According to the U.S. Bureau of Labor Statistics, over half of the working women of the United States are still confined to twenty percent of the 440 occupational categories that this country has to offer.[50] Even in categories traditionally associated with women, men are given the upper-echelon positions or command higher wages for the same work. In 1928, for instance, women were fifty-five percent of the elementary school principals in this country. By 1980, though they remained eighty-four percent of all elementary school teachers, only eleven percent of the elementary school principals of the nation and only four percent of the secondary school principals were women.

The *New York Times* reported in January 1987 that, even at academic institutions with doctoral-level programs, women professors earned an average of $5,000 less than their male counterparts.[51] So much for the greenwood of intellectual awareness and egalitarian philosophy.

Even the Scholastic Aptitude Test upon which scholarship awards and college admission processes depend is skewed to the experiences and education and socialization procedures of young males. Though first year college women regularly earn higher grades than males the same age, they average sixty-one points lower than boys on the SAT. As a result, women get less financial support or academic recognition in their struggle for the education they need to equalize their professional standing.[52]

As a result of this historic lack of financial, educational and developmental support along with discriminatory legislation governing insurance, pension and promotion policies, elderly women are the poorest of the poor and young women are yet to be commonly accepted in top executive positions that bring economic possibility and future security.

The facts cry to heaven for vengeance. In a world that wraps itself in a mantle of male chivalry, women have been left without resources and without concern for their own personal human development. If they do not accept the dependent roles that a male hierarchy has determined for them, they are disadvantaged at every point. If they do accept the dependent roles they've been told are the will of God for them, they are still likely to be left in poverty, without pension monies or a full share of their husband's social security benefits. If they suffer a divorce, the average alimony payment in this country will be $2,800 per year or $2,000 in annual child care payment, not per child but per year, in a country that estimates that it takes $72,000 to raise every single child to the age of eighteen.

Indeed, women have been kept but they have not, as a class, been nurtured in this male-oriented world.

Integrative Power. In a final category, May describes the kind of power that is devoted to mutual concern. Exploitation, competition and manipulation are all intent on self-development at the expense of another. Nurturant power works for others to the point of spending the self for the development of the other. Integrative power, on the other hand, works with others for the sake of the development of both parties. Integrative power is power used to bring unlike needs into unity. It synthesizes the needs of both parties into one great organic whole. It sets out to unify and synthesize and empower. Integrative power is power used to create a whole new world where relationships are formed out of both need and gift and no one is expected to lose.

In a group that functions on integrative power, there is not simply a concern for the development of the other, there is the clear intention to bring the other into the system for the sake of the system itself.

The civil rights movement is an instance of integrative power. Both blacks and whites worked together to achieve integration, not simply so that black society could be better but so that white society could be better as well. The point was not to make the black world decent and the white world safe; the point was to honor the gifts of the other and to make the two worlds one. In the peace movement, the goal is not to defeat the enemy by non-violent means; the purpose of the peace movement is to turn enemies into friends. The peace movement does not simply call for restraint from the parties involved in conflict; it calls for understanding and respect for the rights and visions of everyone concerned. The United Nations is an attempt to bring governments beyond their national borders to recognize the overriding interests of the entire globe.

Integrative power, in other words, is based on structures of collaboration, the ability to work with others as equals, the intention to listen and to learn from one another. In an integrative society, ethnic pluralism, not the melting pot, becomes the ideal. In an integrative church, national churches, not the Roman Church alone, become the face and the norm of the Catholic world and charism. In integrative relationships, the needs and convenience of one member of the pair does not, as a matter of course, supersede the needs and convenience of the other. In integrative power, one element does not consume or control the other. They both become something new, something beyond themselves, together.

Integrative power is based on the assumption that there are multiple rights in society with equal claim for attention and support. The assumption is that rights in tension are rights to be honored, not threats to be suppressed or defeated or ignored.

The theology of integrative power is the theology of the Holy Spirit, which breathes where it wills. If indeed the divine spark is in us all, then the Holy Spirit has outrageously free rein to inspire and inspirit and embody the will of God anywhere. In anyone. Down goes the notion that Indians aren't human. Down goes the concept that blacks aren't fit matter for ordination. Down goes the idea that the church is monolithic or that theology is only European or that economic control is a western prerogative. The fact is that the theology of the Holy Spirit says that fullness of life is a universal holding that is the province of all for the sake of all. More than that, the theology of the Holy Spirit implies that we must bring to reality the oneness that we already share.

Integrative power is power used in such a way that power is not taken away from another in the exercise of it. Unilateral power, no matter how well-intentioned, breeds insensitivity to whatever it touches. As long as we know what is good for the other, there is no reason to really get to know the other, or to listen to the other, or to learn from the other. Integrative power, in other words, is not practiced by having long discussions with the people we are legislating for or by writing pastorals about them or by finally coming to acknowledge their existence in trivial or condescending ways. Integrative power assumes that each of us has a power that is needed by the other and then sets out to work together, as equals, to enable it.

The function of integrative power is to bring opposites together, to bind the factions of the world into one, to tear down the national boundaries and ethnic differences and human distinctions that separate us so that we can all be something new together.

Job's daughters, amorphous and blurred and faceless throughout the story, come into relief in the final chapter of a book that describes the conversion of a man from past theological error to a fullness of understanding of God. Job comes to see how narrow his idea of God and creation and life has been. Job comes to realize that God is not a captive of our misconceptions and our rationalizations and our weaknesses. God is the Other, the one who does not think as we do or act the way we do or shrink life to the narrowed dimensions that we do.

Integrative power is the power that gives us the opportunity to make life whole again.

Women and Integrative Power. As long as divisions based on gender exist anywhere in society, there is no chance for full integration of peoples. The theology of domination, the notion that one part of humanity is more fully human than any other part, implies that

44

inequity and hierarchy are built right into the human race by God. Job was told that suffering was the will of God imposed for sin. Women are told that suffering is the will of God imposed for femaleness. Differences then become the stuff on which control is based rather than the treasure upon which wholeness is built. Differences become the raw material of distinctions and segregation and spiritual slavery. Differences become the justification for suppression of peoples in the name of God. In the nineteenth century this obligation to inflict superiority on the rest of the human race was called "the white man's burden." The fact is that the burden was laid on the backs of non-white men and all women everywhere.

Integration depends on an ability to see all of life as graced and all of life as important and all of life as equal and none of life as beneath us. The problem is that men are socialized to dominate; women are socialized to comply. As a result, it is not only women who are suffering from sexism. Sexism, the notion of male domination, is affecting society in general as well. Women become locked into submissive roles, true, but men become locked in as well to performance and competition and aggression and dominance and responsibility and the need to succeed. The catechism of sexual inequality leads, as a result, to authoritarianism which leads to social violence which depends on a theology of domination and a commitment to an obedience designed to bind some, but not all. The ultimate results are plain to see in the colonialism, nationalism and militarism that even now are dividing the globe rather than integrating it.

Clearly, power is a complex quantity, a charism to be used with care and a quality to be rigorously evaluated. The problem is that power is seldom evaluated at all. It is more likely to be called God's will or the common good or the natural law. It is a quantity hoarded by some and a quality denied to half the human race.

In the meantime, the myth of female privilege continues to cloud the situation and confuse the issue. Why would women want to lose the power they have in being powerless and cared for and supported? Everyone knows the "behind-every-great-man-lies-a-great-woman" argument. Isn't that power of spirit enough for woman? Why would they want what men have?

The answer is simple. In the first place, if power can be defined as the ability to shape the world according to your personal point of view, then women do not have power at all. At best, they may have moral suasion over those willing to be persuaded by them. What they do not have, except in minor or isolated instances, is either the right or the resources to make bad situations better. They can only hope and, of course, pray. In the second place, it is no "privilege" at all to be allowed to be submissive, excitable, dependent, vulnerable, overly sensitive and easily influenced, all traits attributed to women and all traits considered the least socially desirable in test after test of social norms and responses.

In Elizabeth Moss Kantor's studies of men and women in business, the findings are very sobering. Opportunity, power and tokenism, Kantor finds, affect the attitudes of men just as much as those of women. Lack of opportunity, lack of power and showcase tokenism have a negative effect on creativity and morale.[53]

46

The study is based on assumptions about women that have pervaded the social world for centuries. The idea is that since women are by nature suited to the domestic dimensions of life, any other roles will fail either to engage them or to satisfy them. Women belong in the home caring for children and devoted to housework, the study posits, and nothing else really makes them happy. By nature, then, they have lower aspirations than men and, as a class, have less commitment to non-domestic work in general. Women, the popular mythology goes, are more concerned with friendships developed in the workplace than with the work itself. And, clearest of all, women make poor leaders because their personalities simply do not allow them to be assertive. They lack the character traits it takes, in other words, to exercise power properly. They avoid success and they cannot handle people.

Kantor discovers, however, that all of these assumptions are true of both men and women in positions of blocked opportunity or when they find themselves in positions of limited power and responsibility.

It is opportunity itself, Kantor finds, that generates self-esteem, ambition and commitment. Roles without the reward of self-development, therefore, have a universally negative effect on people, all people, men as well as women. Parallel studies moreover conclude that men in routine jobs behaved in exactly the same way that women do in similar situations: they defined the job as "temporary"; they dreamed of leaving it; they adopted values that rationalized the reality of their roles. They liked "easy work," they said, or they preferred to spend time with their families.

47

The process of learning to like what you can't avoid is, it seems, not a gender-related response. Power determines a person's self-definition and direction, of course. It may also define what they give back to society.

Dead-ends, Kantor determined as well, lead people to focus on work-relationships and social situations rather than on task accomplishment or achievement. Being well-liked itself becomes a form of success. Men as well as women become more people-oriented, more "relational" when their environment blocks any other applications of their abilities. The whole idea, then, of women's greater capacity for interpersonal relationships may be more an instance of selective development than of natural propensity.

Finally, Kantor concluded, dead-end jobs generate a self-fulfilling prophecy: since there is no hope, people give up hope. Since there is nothing to desire, people at a dead-end have no desires. The situation is insidious. When workers lower their aspirations to match their environment, employers conclude that they aren't capable of doing more. But if they never get the opportunity to do more, they will never raise their aspirations.

The studies put both ghettos and sexism in a completely different light. It becomes harder to say that people are where they are because of what they are. The possibility is that people are where they are because there is simply no way out for them. We begin to see that personal power breeds personal success and that success breeds personal power. To deprive people of power may be to deprive them of full human growth as well. The fact is that we don't really know if women are powerless because they lack personal power or because they have never had the power to resist powerlessness.

Power, the ability to back up demands, implement programs, influence upper echelons, and reward co-workers, is largely lacking for women who find themselves locked into roles without scope both in the home and outside of it.

Lack of power, some social scientists suggest, may affect personality development as well. Burleigh Gardner, for one, concludes that the powerless become petty and tyrannical and perfectionist in order to protect their own image and position, undesirable as it may be.[54] And sure enough, men without power, the researchers conclude, behave just as weakly as women do and women with real power behave just as well—or just as badly—as men do.

In fact, traditional sex-typing is simply basically unhealthy for both men and women. High femininity, the studies point out, leads to high anxiety, low self-esteem, and low self-acceptance. High masculinity, on the other hand, results in high anxiety, high neuroticism and low self-acceptance.[55] In the samples studied, "masculine" men were found to lack the ability to express warmth, to be playful and to be concerned about others. So-called "feminine women," on the other hand, lacked independence in judgment and the ability to assert their own preferences. The full development of the self and the opportunity to use personal power, in other words, is essential to the mental health of the entire society. In fact, since the advent of the women's movement and its unleashing of the power of women, a report of the Psychiatry Department of the Columbia

49

College of Physicians and Surgeons documents, women are now no more likely to suffer some form of nervous breakdown than men of the same age.[56]

Seen from these perspectives, it becomes imperative that women be given the same kinds of opportunities to develop and succeed as men take for granted or not only will their own souls wither and die but so will they wither the environment around them.

The central question, then, is not whether or not women lack power or whether or not women are capable of exercising power, or whether or not the proper use of power is essential to the development and preservation of the globe. The question is whether or not, in the face of so much liberation theology and so much data, women of this time are indeed so much better off than they have been in the past? The question, too, is whether or not, if the development of women is indeed a natural movement of the spirit, there are instances of it anywhere else on the globe. Is the woman's movement really only a phenomenon of middle-class, over-educated and rebellious women of the western world in revolt against the natural order of things or are there tracings in other societies as well, and if so are the agendas the same? What kind of power is being exercised in behalf of women now around this high technology, philosophically enlightened and sophisticated world?

Equality does not lie in being either too revered or too reviled. Both situations are unreal. The measure of equality is respect. When Job's world finally became whole, it had a feminine focus as well as a male model. The question is: Are Job's daughters honored with respect anyplace in the world now? Is there anywhere where things are in male-female balance, where equality is, where power, real power, belongs to all the people, both female and male. And if not, why not? And what does that say to western feminists, male and female alike?

Women and Power: An International Agenda

A rising body of information gives clear evidence of two things: first, the woman's movement for personal power is a global one; second, the woman's agenda, though universal in some ways, is also unique from region to region. Feminism in the United States is a piece of, but not all of, the issues that women as women must deal with worldwide.

The problem is that women's issues in the third world are often seen merely as political issues if they are seen at all. In Haiti, for instance, roads are a woman's issue because women are the ones who are responsible for getting the family crops up and down the mud-rut mountains to market. In Mexico, water is a woman's issue because it is women who travel hours every day to fetch the family water from wells that have long been dry. In Africa, agricultural policy is a woman's issue because it is women who have been forced out of food production by western development policies.

It is these issues, in other words, that are forgotten in development programs, not because they do not have something to do with development but because they are labeled "women's issues," and therefore not important to the males of the society, either native or western.

The one constant from continent to continent is the fact of women's subjection and domination and disproportionate universal deprivation. For feminists to begin to make a worldwide impact, however, they must begin to understand one another. They must begin to see the world through one another's eyes.

The conflict theorist Gaetano Mosca argued that whenever any social force—money, land, military organization, religion, education, labor, science, anything —becomes significant to the society, those who hold high positions in this new social force must be incorporated into the ruling class of the culture.[57] Women, it is apparent, are noticeably lacking in every administrative system in the world. Only ten percent of high government officials are women; only five percent of the CEO's of the business world are women; no percentage at all of the hierarchy or even of the clerical estate of the Roman Catholic Church are women. If Mosca is correct, then the social valuation of women is clearly negative, if there is a social valuation at all.

National proverbs of ancient vintage confirm the theory: "A wife married is like a pony bought; I'll ride her and whip her as I like," the Chinese say. "No matter how skilled a women may be in mathematics, her judgment will always be second rate," they say in Sri Lanka. "I thought I saw two people but it was only a man and his wife," they say in Russia. "Does your wife work? No, she just stays at home," they say in Africa. "Woman and soil both improve with beating," they say in Asia. The temptation, of course, is to dismiss such folklore on the grounds that it is the residue of a time long past and a people who were poorly prepared. The facts, however, dash the hope.

World Watch Institute, an international research organization, set out in 1988 to describe the problems faced by women around the world in the course of maternity care.[58] What the researchers discovered is that despite the issues of malnutrition, poverty, unemployment and health facing women in the third world, what women identified repeatedly as the most serious problem they had to deal with was the issue of domestic violence, wife-beating, physical brutality. Women, it seems, are universally devalued and universally disadvantaged. Everywhere, power is used against women even today, ten years after the U.N. Decade on Women.

The woman's agenda is not, however, a simple one. Tradition, religion and culture all conspire to make the concerns of women everywhere the same and everywhere different.

In India, the second largest nation in the world with a population of over three hundred million women, the preamble of the Constitution of the Republic defines the nation as a welfare state dedicated to the pursuit of socio-economic justice, and Article 15 of the Constitution prohibits discrimination on the grounds of religion, race, caste, place of birth or sex.[59] The obstacles confronting the accomplishment of these ideals, however, are formidable.

The employment of women has declined steadily with the introduction of the western process of "modernization." The educational and economic opportunities which, ironically, appear to motivate a reduction in birthrates and a rise in the standard of living is largely denied to women in India. The power used to control women for the sake of the social order, in other words, is exactly what is contributing to a breakdown in the social order.

The Laws of Manu defined a position of total legal dependence of females on males similar to the strictures found in Confucian law, Roman law and the English Doctrine of Coverture.

The law is clear:

A wife, a son and a slave, these three are ever ordained destitute of property; whatever they acquire becomes his property whose they are (Manu I, 147).

In childhood a female must be subject to her father, in youth to her husband, and when her lord is dead, to her sons; a woman must never be independent (Manu I, 149).

Manu also forbade the remarriage of widows, developed the institution of child marriage, and held up *sati*, or widow burning, as an ideal. The control of women was complete. Economic power was entirely in the hands of men, and women had lost all independent status.

To this day, in traditional families, women are deferential not only to their husbands but to all adult males. Marriages are arranged at an early age. Widowhood is a dreaded condition. The widow has no right to property and, worse, she is often blamed for her husband's death. Her usefulness is over and she is considered a polluting force in society. Under these conditions *sati* becomes a blessing to women left defenseless and destitute by the death of a husband.

British rule challenged at least some of the traditional gender laws but westernization brought a sexism of its own.

Laws enshrining the absolute ownership of private property and the investment of male heads of household with all property rights made the Indian woman just one more piece of property, one more thing to be owned and discarded at will.

The reformer Gandhi saw the emancipation of women as an essential element in the regeneration of India. "We must be incapable of defending ourselves or healthily competing with other nations, if we allow the better half of ourselves to become paralyzed," he said.[60]

The emphasis of Indian reformers, however, was on a gender equality that was complementary but different. As a result, for the Indian woman emancipation became simply a new form of control. Throughout the twentieth century, women's participation in the Indian workforce has actually declined. While male employment increased by fifteen percent, the percentage of female workers decreased by forty-one percent. In agriculture where the farm equipment provided by the west has been routinely given to men rather than to women, the figures are even worse. The unemployment rate is twice as high among women agricultural laborers as it is for men and their number of days worked are lower. Yet women agricultural workers are the largest single category of Indian working women. Eighty percent of all women who work for wages, about one-third of the total agricultural labor force, work on farms. Worst of all, options are scarce—about ninety-five percent of the women farmworkers are illiterate—and public aid for women is non-existent.

The picture of the Indian woman, therefore, is a grave one. She may be championed as equal but she is not treated as equal. She is treated as a domestic servant whose role in life is simply to cater to the needs of men, whose death may well be blamed on her bad *karma* or female spirit. She has little chance for economic self-reliance. She is seen as an economic burden. Last year in Bombay alone, of the 8,000 recorded abortions, 7,999 were of female fetuses. And all the while, the process of industrial development and agricultural development favors men with jobs and equipment and established salary scales while women recede further and further into the background.

Obviously, what men call development does not necessarily produce improvement in the status of women. Power, as Mosca points out, goes to the powerful.[61] The continuing development of a commercial market economy with machine-driven production has caused the displacement of farmers, increased rural poverty, and migration. At the same time, low technology, labor-intensive craft sectors where women workers predominate have been replaced by even more industrialized processes. Women in service industries, such as market sellers, are in increasing competition with mass-marketing systems. And all of these with no compensating protection or welfare support for the women themselves.

Modernization, in other words, as the experience in India shows, not only displaces women but also works to hold women in place, or leave them behind, as men primarily reap the benefits of education, political participation and the new employment opportunities designed by men and for men. In India, westernization is a feminist issue and all of western power is arrayed with the power of tradition to keep women in the place that men say they should be.

In addition to economic oppression, moreover, women in India today still bear the burdens of traditionalism and male backlash. For instance, no uniform legal code governs marriage and inheritance laws in India.

Worse, though dowry-giving has been declared against the law, it is not "a cognizable offense," one subject to judicial hearing and decision. The laws, in other words, are not enforced. Dowry deaths, the murder of a woman whose dowry is considered inadequate, are on the rise. In 1987 the police officially recorded 1,786 dowry deaths in all of India—murders committed by husbands unsatisfied with the dowry given or seeking to profit from another one—but the Ahmedabad Women's Action Group estimates that 1,000 women were burned alive in the state of Gujurat alone. And mortality data from India reveals that nineteen percent of all deaths among women 15–44 years of age are due to "accidental burns." World Watch Institute reports that, by contrast, the same figure is less than one percent in Guatemala, Ecuador and Chile, clear indications that the "accidents" are no accidents at all.[62]

To be a woman, in other words, is to be at the mercy of the power group to which she has no access and whose talk of chivalry is condemned by the realities of her life.

And it is everywhere the same. Religious tradition has declared women dependent and complementary and modernization has shunted her to an underclass that is unemployed, undervalued, illiterate and forgotten. And all for reasons Job would well recognize: moral incapacity and the will of God.

In China, the Confucian state which prevailed from the sixth century permeated Chinese political theory and defined all social relationships.[63] In this man-centered society where women were considered a threat to family loyalty and property, the subordination of women was necessary for the system to succeed. If the relationship between husband and wife were too strong, in other words, he might be more devoted to her and her concerns than to his family. He might give her their property. He might listen to her and do more what she wanted him to do than what they wanted him to do.

To assure the continuation of the family line, women were made perpetual legal minors. They passed from the control of their fathers to their husbands, and upon widowhood, to their sons. A woman could never act autonomously. Women who ran away could be beaten or sold if caught.

Taoism, another former of Chinese culture, taught

that the universe is sustained by the interaction of opposites—*yin,* the female principle, and *yang,* the male principle. *Yin* they defined as passive, *yang* as active, light and good. According to this way of thinking female inferiority is natural and inherent.

Both Confucian and Taoist concepts were used to justify and maintain the subordination of women. Female infanticide was widespread and marriage was a contract between families, not individuals. Men had the right to divorce a woman for childlessness, negligence in serving his parents, stealing, adultery, disease or talkativeness. Women had no divorce rights at all. Polygamy was a common way to achieve both male heirs and social status. Footbinding gave men both erotic satisfaction and the assurance that their women would be passive and controllable.

A demand for free-choice marriages, equal treatment before the law, the abolition of concubinage and footbinding, and widow remarriage became crucial issues in the Chinese feminist movement of the nineteenth and twentieth centuries. Some women began to take vows not to marry; others committed suicide to escape their torment.

Finally, as it had in India, the efforts to emancipate women were greatly enhanced by the rising current of nationalism in China.

Mao Tse-tung wrote, "China's women are a vast reserve of labor power. This reserve should be tapped," he said, "and used in the struggle to build a mighty socialist country."[64] Mao stressed labor-intensive production techniques to counter the technologically superior west. Power apparently had passed to the masses, women and men alike. Women, it seemed, would be a direct beneficiary of the system.

In the rural areas of China, though, custom and prevailing notions of the natural inferiority of women have outwitted change. Betrothal gifts from the family of the groom to the family of the bride still mark the marriage as a contract between families and an exchange of properties.

In the communes, domestic labor, unlike other forms of communal service, is unpaid and produces a dependent class of women. Work-point accounting is by household and payments are made only to its male head. Since women have no right to dispose of money without the permission of their husbands, women lack the crucial power of economic control that leads to independence.

Sex-role differentiation in jobs is common and women's work receives lower work-points than men's.[65] So, of course, female infanticide is common due to the "one-child family" system imposed by the government to control birth rates in China. In the first place, sons are more valuable economically; in the second place, many Chinese still believe that without a son, there can be no descendants.

In the most professedly egalitarian of societies, in other words, discrimination against women has been imposed by the male power structure to maintain the privileges that go with control. The power to write the laws, to implement the laws and to teach the laws has operated to circumvent the possibilities of a whole people. So convinced have women been of their own inferiority and functional role in society that they have become their own jailers. What is willed by God and essential to society is not, after all, easily to be rejected.

The fact is that women in China have, like the rest of the women of the world, been the recipients of some good-willed favors, perhaps, but they have not been given the most important quality of all, the power to change things themselves.

In Oceania—Polynesia, Melanesia, and Micronesia—religious systems all stress the notion that men are superior and that women are to submit to male control, for their own good, of course.[66] Men are considered sacred; women, "common." Men still control marriage transactions and with it the development and destinies of women. And as it did everywhere, no matter what their traditional roles, colonization routinely diminished whatever status native women did have. Bell writes about the conditions of Pacific women:

> Women were disadvantaged from the outset because of the white male perception of them as domestic workers and sex objects. Aboriginal men have been able to take real political advantage of certain aspects of frontier society, while aboriginal women have been seen by whites as peripheral to the political process.[67]

In general, the introduction of a wage economy has had different effects on the condition of women than it has had on the conditions of men. It has changed their relationship both to the economic structures of the society and to one another. In the wage economy introduced by western colonialism, men gain

61

stature and power; women move into the labor force in menial capacities. Family structure changes with migration to urban centers and women find themselves with increased family responsibility and decreased economic control.

For women in colonized territories it is hard to make a case for the superiority of western ways or for the fact that they themselves have been benefited by it.

In Africa, too, societies in which women once enjoyed importance as farmers, traders, spirit mediums, chiefs and even warriors, colonialism and modernization have greatly eroded the status, influence and authority of women.[68]

Marriage and family relationships in Africa had traditionally served more to develop the clan and to cement political alliances than to provide emotional control. Marriage was a way to achieve social status, to acquire children and to establish partnerships with sexually defined divisions of labor more than it was the giving of women to men. Bridewealth, the transfer of goods in compensation for the transfer of female labor and reproductive power through marriage, and brideservice, the practice of having a suitor contribute several years of labor to the woman's clan before marriage to pay for their loss in her, discriminated against women by giving the men control but it did not signify ownership. It was simply considered necessary to create the contractual obligations that marriage implied for both parties.

Bridewealth and brideservice established the right to incorporate all children born during the marriage into the legal husband's lineage, regardless of their actual paternity or subsequent divorce. It did not signify the purchase of the wife as chattel; it established obligations between the man and woman, unequal perhaps but reciprocal nevertheless. Women did not lose their names or family identities or become domestic slaves without pay. Often, in fact, marriage was matrilineal. The husband moved in with the kin of the wife and authority rested more with her brothers than with the new husband. Co-wives were often welcomed to increase the wife's freedom to farm or trade on her own account by having separate homesteads where the burdens of child care and household services owed to the husband could be shared.

The point is that the economic position of women in many traditional African societies was much stronger than in most other cultures. Women were usually the primary producers in hoe agriculture and they dominated local trade and markets in many areas. A substantial part of the married woman's agricultural production was owed to her husband and children but the profits she made from trading were commonly regarded as her own. It was not unusual, consequently, for women to become independently wealthy even though men controlled the land and dominated the most profitable sectors of the economy.

With the advent of the westernization of Africa and the introduction of manufactured goods, women have lost their role as chief suppliers of domestic goods and the trading system that went with it. Trade and marketing have become the province of men and with them the profits they imply. Development planning, thought to be for the common good, has in fact either completely ignored or at least harmed women's interests. Since independence, the definition of "head of household" as exclusively male in census data and planning projects has largely excluded women from participation in any major program.

Worse, children have become a new kind of economic burden in an economy where the cost of raising children to take their place in a cash economy has become more and more difficult to provide. Finally, the stability of marriage has fallen prey to urban industry and the mobility required of the men who must travel to the cities for employment. And with it all, women have become more and more isolated, more and more vulnerable, more and more neglected and more and more poor.

With the westernization of economic systems and political processes in Africa has come a whole new set of women's agendas—land, water, fuel and food—all called development problems in the first world but all really women's problems in this part of the world and all seen as the legacy of imperialism, colonialism and westernization. The power to develop some has become the power to destroy the rest, the women.

In Latin America the traditional norm of passivity and dependence is underscored even more by the machismo philosophy that makes women a sex object and domestic servant.[69] In a machismo society, men strive for many sexual conquests and many children while women are relegated to the home. Men practice serial monogamy; that is, they live with one woman at a time but with few women forever, abandoning their mates and children without support or the personal resources of education or welfare to sustain them in an overpopulated society with no lack of labor force.

In situations such as these, women are the most exploited of workers, subject always in all things—their social life, their educational endeavors, their work choices—to the will of their husbands. Evelyn P. Stevens goes so far as to argue that Latin America will not experience a feminist movement equivalent to the organizations of women in post-industrial societies unless the consistent and continued total exploitation of women legislated by the state and affirmed by the church can be changed.[70]

Latin American women, in an attempt to escape total control, either do not marry young or choose not to marry at all. Eighteen percent of women in Latin America between the ages of thirty and sixty-four are single. Many others function in multiple-mate relationships to gain financial support and a certain amount of independence at the same time.[71]

Industrialization, which increases the number of middle-class families who need servants, and agribusiness, which drives people off the land, fuel the rise of an underpaid domestic servanthood, basically female, in the absence of other job opportunities.[72] In situations like this, women without education or privilege are driven to accept the lowest of low wages and unstable working conditions. In the meantime, U.S. industries exploit the situation of unmarried or poor women by transferring their industries south of the border. They do not transfer, however, the wage scales or pension benefits or medical assistance programs that characterize those same industries in the United States.[73]

Again, the effects of office, tradition, custom and ideology in Latin America are loaded against women. In the poorest of societies, women are always the poorest of the poor with little or no resources to change the situation. And all the powers of the world—philosophy, religion, and law—are mustered against them.

The debate about women's roles in Islamic countries turns on which *hadiths* or laws about women are to be believed to be truly the sayings of the prophet Mohammed and how they are to be interpreted.[74] Most scholars agree that Mohammed's views on women, polygamy, property rights and inheritance were progressive for the time, but later interpretations by male ideologues embodied inequality and restriction into the legal codes of the area. Whether or not some of the other early laws regarding women or the works which interpret them were also of Mohammed's design is of considerable dispute among Islamic scholars. Whatever the case, Islamic women have been subject to multiple restrictions in the name of religion which persist to this day.

Women, for instance, have traditionally not been considered equal to men in family law. They inherit only one-half the share of the men in the family. Child custody, vested in the mother during childhood, reverts to the father after the child reaches a certain age, earlier for boys than for girls. Divorce laws are inequitable and women are directed by numerous religious injunctions on modesty and obedience to men. The Sunni Fundamentalist perspective, for instance, argues that male control of women and their *purdah* or seclusion is divinely ordained and indispensable to the proper functioning of society.[75]

Though "equal in the eyes of God," the cultural status of separate-and-unequal ultimately took sway. Over the years women lost their right even to pray in mosques or to become religious scholars.[76] Seclusion, the veil, clitoridectomy and infibulation are all linked with cultural concepts of family honor. Women are defined in the culture as sexually aggressive and, therefore, likely to behave dishonorably if left alone with men. The economic implications of protecting inheritance lines and controlling the transfer of property is, of course, no small part of the concept. To this day, as a result of the ideology and the property concerns, the female's sexual honor is to be protected by seclusion, announced by the veil, guarded by her male relatives at all costs, and, if violated, can result in the death of the woman herself.

Genital mutilation, the excision of female genitalia in order to eliminate a woman's capacity for sexual pleasure and insure female monogamy, is not required by the Koran and has been present in other cultures as well as the Islamic. Clitoridectomy, for instance, was also practiced by physicians in nineteenth century Europe and was recommended even later than that to "cure" certain "female disorders" as well as nymphomania, hysteria, depression and epilepsy. It has, nevertheless, flourished in Muslim areas and results in medical and sexual complications of the most profound degree, even death.[77]

The United Nations World Health Organization

reported in 1985 that over eighty million instances of female mutilation had been documented in Africa alone.[78] Without it, women become unmarriageable, rejected and poor. The price, then, of femaleness in these areas is the loss of femaleness itself. The price of male pride and control is total loss of autonomy, public participation and full human development for women.

Lack of participation in the public arena, lack of economic independence, lack of entry into the public sphere, low female participation even in agriculture and the loss to industrialization of women's informal market system and home industries—sewing, weaving, embroidery, factory piece work, garden vegetables, kitchen products, small animal husbandry and midwifery —have led to an even greater devaluation of women and their work.

Finally, current world events—the Arab-Israeli conflict, the Arab defeat in the Seven Day War and the U.S. support of Israel—have all led to a surge of traditionalism. Feminism, therefore, is equated with westernism and seen as a type of national treason or immorality. As a result, Arab women find themselves taking up the veil again to distance themselves from the criticisms of westernism both as an affirmation of the dignity of women and as a sign of their indigenous roots.[79]

The position of feminists in the Arab world is one fraught with politics, tied to nationalism and obstructed by religious tradition and the on-going wars of the region, the results of which fall heaviest on refugee women, illiterate and poor, who get little or no support from the men whose war it is.

The questions, obviously, are worldwide. The questions, clearly, are far-ranging. The questions called political are often feminist. The questions, of course, are questions of power and they are legion: Can "separate" ever truly be "equal"? Who defines who will be "protected"? On what grounds? For whose advantage? At whose request? But without the power to force the discussion, how will women ever get the questions answered from a woman's perspective as long as ideology, office and law are controlled by men and applied from the male perspective?

Without a doubt, exploitation, competition and manipulation of women are everywhere the national policy, the legal expectation, the ideological ideal.

A NEW WORLD VISION: JOB'S DAUGHTERS

What is threatening about the woman's movement is not that the woman's movement is changing the domestic role of women. What is threatening about the woman's movement is that it challenges the very foundations upon which power is based in every institution in society.

Like Job, women know that the inhuman and the unequal and the unfair simply cannot be the will of God.

Like Job, who confronted God to discover the reason for his suffering only to find out that there was no reason, feminist theologians and philosophers and biologists and psychologists are confronting the systems that restrain them only to discover that there is no real reason for the disempowerment of women across the world except the disempowering power structures of men.

And, like Job, women know that things must be changed if God is going to be allowed to be God.

The symbol of Job's new world is the symbol of Job's three daughters—Dove, Cinnamon and Eye-Shadow, the translators call them—not invisible now, but named, not dependent but propertied, not faceless but uniquely gentle, personable and female. In Job's new world, the feminine is very present and just as powerful, just as established, just as influential as her brothers are. Job's new world, in other words, is the world turned upside down. In this world, equality does not diminish resources, it doubles them. In this world, the development of women does not diminish men, it enhances them. In this world, conflict is not the basis of security and peace and feminism does not signal weakness; it secures the strength of every one.

That world is yet to come for women.

During the United Nations Decade for Women, 1975–85, efforts were made around the globe to lift the suffering of women and to improve their political, economic and social standing.[80] Ninety percent of the governments of the world now have official bodies devoted to the advancement of women and over half of those have been set up during the decade. More important, perhaps, we now have more documentation and data on the condition of women than the world has ever known or even cared to ask.

And advances were certainly made. Some laws were changed. Some new levels of education were reached. Some employment opportunities were made available. Some health care facilities were improved. Some new levels of social and political participation were reached. Nevertheless, throughout the world, women are still a disproportionately large percentage of the poor, the illiterate, the abused, the unemployed and the underemployed. Most of all, they hold a disproportionately small percentage of the world's real political power. And they still do more work for less pay and fewer benefits than any men of any region of the world. But these things will not change until men change their own systems.

Worse, the effects of the world debt crisis, industrialization, national export strategies, foreign aid policies, multi-national production processes, and the imbalance between military and social spending all fall most heavily on the backs of women.

The world debt crisis forces debtor nations to introduce austerity measures in the society that make development programs impossible in order to meet debt service to the richest nations in the world. A country beholden to foreign debt cannot put in roads to markets or build schools or educate teachers or lay water lines. As a result women are isolated, illiterate and forced to walk for miles and hours every day just to get the water they need to do the rest of their work. Indeed, it is women who suffer most from the loss of

71

government supports or services and it is women who have no power to change the situation.

Industrialization displaces agricultural workers of which women are the majority and eliminates the home industries and markets that have long been the economic staple of women in third world countries.

National export strategies call for the production by third world countries of cash crops to satisfy western markets in exchange for American trade favors or capital investment. In the eighty-three poorest countries of the world, three percent of the landowners own eighty percent of the land.[81] More and more fertile land, in other words, is being taken away from peasant farmers. As a result, women lose the support of subsistence farming and find themselves unemployed and at the mercy of an expensive import system for the basics of life.

Foreign aid policies that give technology, land and money to men only, even in areas where the industry being developed has traditionally been woman's work, have upset the social balance of whole societies and left women without both status and employment.

Multi-national corporations that move assembly plants of first world products to third world nations for cheap labor exploit a whole new generation of poor and displaced women in sweat shops of the twentieth century. In Haiti, women earn three to four dollars a day for making baseballs for all National League teams, a grueling task that involves pulling single length threads over nine feet long through leather over and over again without pause in order to meet the quota of thirty-six baseballs a day. Otherwise, the women lose their jobs and the little they have.

Rising military expenditures deprive development programs of billions of dollars. In the United States under the Reagan administration alone, six billion dollars were taken from social welfare programs benefiting women and children in order to develop the military-industrial complex, despite the fact that public poll after public poll showed that women wanted military spending reduced overall, and despite the fact that the elimination of only one Trident nuclear submarine of a proposed fleet of fifteen would have restored full food stamp benefits to all of the 15.9 million women who were food stamp recipients at that time.[82]

At the same time in third world countries, one-half to two-thirds of the women are anemic with no health care programs to rely on and little food to live on.

In the light of these realities for women, in both the third world and the first, the U.N. Decade for Women named three daughters of its own—peace, development and equality—who must be recognized, honored and freed if a new world for women is ever to come.

Peace. Without peace the development of women is impossible. Militarism saps our best minds, our best resources and the bulk of our finances for the sake of destruction, without putting anything of value back into society and by providing only a small number of jobs for only the highest of high-skilled workers.

Worse, militarism only feeds the notion of sex-role

stereotypes. Male dominance, masculine values and "machoism" all thrive in a military culture. Women become the booty of war, its refugees and victims. In the United States alone, in what we insist is a peacetime economy, to increase the military budget for weapons procurement, we cut Medicaid, Aid to Families with Dependent Children, and the Child Nutrition Program, all programs of great importance to women.

Until violence against women is stamped out, the attitudes that breed it will continue to thrive and silently, insidiously, undergird every male-female relationship in the world. Until violence against women is rejected by men at every level, every woman is still abused and every man is implicitly involved in the abuse.

Development. Without development programs that involve women and take women's issues into account, the growth and improvement in women's quality of life will be impossible.

Everywhere women have been conditioned to want less, to expect less, and to receive less than men do. As a result they are underpaid, undereducated and underfed; ironically enough, much of the situation has been created in the name of development. Western industrialization took women's jobs, their land, and their social status by putting money, education and technology under the exclusive control of men and identifying only men as "heads of the household" with all the legal rights that implies.

More than sixty percent of the eight hundred million illiterate of the world are women. And in some

74

areas female illiteracy is as high as eighty-five percent.[83] If power lies in the ability to shape ideas, there is no power in that.

Approximately three-fourths of all Korean workers in export industries are female, seventy-two percent of them under the age of twenty-three. They work the longest hours in the industry and earn an average of $65 per month while the men who work with them make $112 for the same kinds of work.[84] If power lies in the ability to use resources to make things happen, there is no power in that.

In the United States, one of the richest countries of the world, fifty percent of all elderly women live on less than $5,000 a year, though less than twenty-five percent of elderly men live on a comparable income.[85] If power lies in the ability to change the laws that control the system, there is no power in that.

The fact is that third world development programs have been based on assumptions that have been disproven. All development programs are not necessarily good for all. Most economic and political changes are not sex-neutral in their effects. The needs of women and the needs of men are not necessarily the same. The participation of women is not simply marginally important to national development. Unless women are included in the organization, planning and decision-making moments of development programs, they and the nation they set out to serve will both suffer.

Equality. Equality means that women must have the same rights, the same responsibilities and the same opportunities that men do. But that can only happen if women have the same power that men do to make the same kinds of decisions, the same kinds of profits, the same kinds of contributions to thought and law and life. Until women become equal partners with men in every office, every home, every shop and every chancery of the world, it will be a myth to talk about the equality of women.

Involvement in politics is a newer thing for women than most people realize. In 1945 only thirty-one countries allowed women the right to vote, and our own only twenty-three years before that date. By 1978, one hundred and twenty-four countries had finally awarded women this basic right. Yet few women in either developed or undeveloped countries have the opportunity to vote for women for public office. But without the power to influence the laws that affect them, people have no power at all.

Power lies in being able to control resources, to make laws, to apply sanctions and to shape ideas. That is the power that women must soon have if the globe itself is not to be brought into jeopardy. Laws must protect women, not enslave them; a dependency theory that makes women minors must be rejected in favor of adulthood; attitudes that feed the notion of women as things and women as helpmates and women as domestic servants and women as the secondary creations of God must change in favor of women as women; religion must not be used as an argument against the glory of God in all creation.

Job came to see God for what God was. Job saw the world, too, for what the world was. And to change things, Job named his daughters: Dove, Cinnamon and Eye-Shadow; the quiet, the dynamic and the feminine; peace, development and equality.

We need a new world, too. We need Job's daughters again.

NOTES

1. Mary A. Scott, *A Woman's Book*. Freedom, CA: The Crossing Press, 1983.
2. Susan Moller Okin, *Women in Western Political Thought*. Princeton: Princeton University Press, 1979.
3. *The Book of Job,* trans. Stephen Mitchell. San Francisco: North Point Press, 1987.
4. Ibid., p. 3.
5. Ibid., p. 6.
6. Ibid., p. 35.
7. Ibid., p. 41.
8. Ibid., p. 44.
9. Ibid., p. 45.
10. Ibid., p. 59.
11. Ibid., p. 58.
12. Ibid., p. 64.
13. Ibid., p. 71.
14. Ibid., p. 91.
15. Ibid.
16. Max Weber, *The Theory of Social and Economic Organization,* ed. Talcott Parsons. New York: Free Press, 1947, pp. 152–153.
17. William Graham Sumner, *Folkways*. New York: New American Library Mentor Books, 1979 (reprint of 1924 ed.).
18. Gaetano Mosca, *The Ruling Class,* trans. Hannah Kahn; ed. and rev. with introduction by Arthur Livingston. New York: McGraw-Hill Book Co., 1939.

19. Rollo May, *Power and Innocence: A Search for the Sources of Violence*. New York: W. W. Norton and Co., Inc., 1972.

20. Herman J. Nieboer, *Slavery as an Industrial System*. Rotterdam: Martinus Nijhoff, 1900, as cited by Dorothy Wertz, Ph.D., "Women and Slavery, a Cross-cultural Perspective," *International Journal of Women's Studies* 7, no. 4, 1984.

21. Ibid.

22. Plato, *Timaeus, Critias, Cleitophon, Menexus, Epistolae* (Loeb Classical Library, No. 238). Cambridge: The Harvard University Press.

23. Plato, *Laws*, trans. T. J. Saunders. New York: Penguin Books, Inc., 1970.

24. Plato, *Timaeus*.

25. Plato, *Theaetetus*, trans. Benjamin Jowett. Indianapolis: Bobbs-Merrill Co., Inc., 1949.

26. Okin, *Political Thought*, p. 82.

27. Thomas Aquinas, *The Summa Theologica*, Vol. I. New York: Benziger Brothers, 1947, pp. 466, 472.

28. Matthew Bacon, *A New Abridgment of the Law*. Dublin: Luke White, 1786, cited by Carol Bauer and Lawrence Ritt, "A Husband Is a Beating Animal—Frances Power Cobbe Confronts Wife-Abuse Problems in Victorian England," *International Journal of Women's Studies*, 6, no. 2, March/April 1983.

29. Ibid.

30. June Stephenson, Ph.D., *Women's Roots*. Napa, CA: Diemer, Smith Publishing Company, Inc., 1988.

31. Plato, *Republic*, trans. Benjamin Jowett. New York: Random House, Inc., 1955.

32. Rita Bornstein, "The Education of Women: Protection or Liberation," *Educational Leadership, Journal of the Association for Supervision and Curriculum Development*, February 1979, pp. 331–337.

33. Ibid.

34. S. Jeremy Hall, O.S.B., "The Character of Benedictine Higher Education" in *The Continuing Quest for God*, ed. William Skudlarek, O.S.B. Collegeville: Liturgical Press, 1981, p. 206.

35. Lori Heise, "Crimes of Gender," *World Watch*, 2, no. 2, March/April 1989.

36. Karl Marx, *Das Kapital*. South Bend: Gateway Editions, Ltd.

37. Weber, *Organization*.

38. Edward Gibbon, *The Decline and Fall of the Roman Empire*, abridged with introduction by F. C. Bourne. New York: Dell Publishing Co., Inc., 1963.

39. Eleanor Emmons Maccoby and Carol Nagy Jacklin, "Myth, Reality and Shades of Gray: What We Know and Don't Know About Sex Differences," *Psychology Today*, December 1974.

40. Michael Kolbenschlag, "Dr. Estelle Ramey: Reclaiming the Feminine Legacy," *Human Behavior*, July 1976, p. 25.

41. P. B. Johnson and J. D. Goodchild, "How Women Get Their Way," *Psychology Today*, October 1976.

42. Maccoby and Jacklin, "Sex Differences."

43. R. David Freedman, "Women, A Power Equal to Man," *Biblical Archeological Review*, 9, no. 1, January/February 1983, pp. 56–58.

44. Emmanuel D'Lorenzo, O.M.I., *Sacrament of Orders* as quoted in "Does the Church Discriminate Against Women on the Basis of Their Sex?" By Catherine Beaton, *Critic*, June–July 1966, pp. 21–27.

45. Mitchell, *Job*, p. 6.

46. Ibid., p. 19.

47. Ibid., p. 25.

48. Ibid., p. 31.

49. Ibid., p. 88.

50. NOW Legal Defense and Education Fund, *The Myth of Equality*. Fact sheet. Washington, D.C., 1983.

51. Larry Rohter, "Women Gain Degrees, but not Tenure," *New York Times,* January 4, 1987.
52. "Today," A Newspaper for the National Education Association, 5, no. 9, June 1987.
53. Elizabeth Moss Kantor, Ph.D., "Why Bosses Turn Bitchy," *Psychology Today,* May 1987.
54. Ibid.
55. Sandra Lipsitz Bem, "Fluffy Women and Chesty Men," *Psychology Today,* September 1975.
56. Phyllis Chester, "Men Drive Women Crazy," *Psychology Today,* July 1971.
57. Mosca, *Ruling Class.*
58. *World Watch,* "Crimes of Gender."
59. Margot I. Duley, "Women in India," *The Cross-cultural Study of Women,* by Margot I. Duley and Mary I. Edwards. New York: The Feminist Press, 1986.
60. Ibid.
61. Mosca, *Ruling Class.*
62. *World Watch,* "Crimes of Gender," p. 15.
63. Margot I. Duley, "Women in China," in Duley and Edwards.
64. Stuart R. Schram, *The Political Thought of Mao Tse-tung.* 2d ed. revised. Baltimore: Penguin Books, 1969, p. 338-339.
65. Duley, *Cross-cultural Study,* pp. 268-269.
66. Karen Sinclair, "Women in Oceania," in Duley and Edwards.
67. Diane Bell, *Daughters of the Dreaming.* Sydney: Allen and Unwin. 1984, in Duley and Edwards, p. 288.
68. Lance F. Morrow, "Women in Sub-Saharan Africa," in Duley and Edwards, p. 290.
69. Muriel Nazzari, "Women in Latin America," in Duley and Edwards, p. 376.
70. Evelyn P. Stevens, "The Prospects for a Women's Liberation Movement in Latin America," *Journal of Marriage and the Family* 35, no. 2, May 1973.

71. Duley and Edwards, pp. 390–391.

72. Laurel Bossen, "Women Modernizing Societies," *American Ethnologist*, 2, 1975.

73. International Labor Rights, Education and Research Foundation. Background paper, May 1989.

74. Margot I. Duley, "Women in the Islamic Middle East and North Africa," in Duley and Edwards.

75. Abdul A'La Maududi, *Purdah and the Status of Women in Islam*, trans. and ed. Al-Ashari. Lahore: Islamic Pub., 1972, as cited by Duley and Edwards.

76. Ignaz Goldziher, *Muslim Studies*, trans. S. M. Stern and C. R. Barber. London: Allen and Unwin, 1970, as quoted by Duley and Edwards, p. 416.

77. Ibid., p. 424.

78. *World Watch*, "Crimes of Gender," p. 18.

79. Nadia H. Youseff, "Cultural Ideals, Feminine Behavior and Family Control," *Comparative Studies in Society and History*, 15, No. 3, June 1973, as cited by Duley and Edwards.

80. United Nations, *Report of the World Conference to Review and Appraise the Achievements of the United Nations Decade for Women: Equality, Development and Peace*. New York: United Nations, 1985.

81. Bread for the World, *Women in Development*. Background paper #29 prepared by Barbara Howell. Washington, D.C., November 1978.

82. SANE, *Military Spending*. Background paper. Washington, D.C., 1983.

83. Global Education Associates, *Breakthrough* 7, no. 4, Summer 1986, p. 9.

84. Bread for the World, *Women in Development*.

85. Women's Research and Education Institute, *Older Women: The Economics of Aging*. Report prepared by Sara E. Rix. Washington, D.C., 1984.

ADDITIONAL SOURCES

1. Ailsa Burns and Ross Homel, "Sex Role Satisfaction Among Australian Children: Some Sex, Age and Cultural Group Comparisons," *Psychology of Women Quarterly,* 10, 1986, pp. 285–96.
2. James T. Duke, *Conflict and Power in Social Life.* Provo, UT: Brigham Young University Press, 1975.
3. Antonia Fraser, *The Warrior Queens.* New York: Alfred A. Knopf, 1989.
4. S. Kleinman, *Equals before God.* Chicago: University of Chicago Press, 1984.
5. Beverly Lindsay, *Comparative Perspectives of Third World Women: The Impact of Race, Sex, and Class.* New York: Praeger Publishers, 1980.
6. Janet Momsen and Janet Townsend (eds.), *The Geography of Gender.* Albany: State University of New York Press, 1987.
7. U.S. Bureau of the Census, Washington, D.C.
8. U.S. Department of Labor, Bureau of Statistics, Washington, D.C.
9. Women's International League for Peace and Freedom. *Arms and the Woman.* Background paper prepared by Naomi Marcus. Philadelphia, 1981.
10. Women's International League for Peace and Freedom. *Balancing the Budget on the Backs of Women.* Report prepared by Debbie Hollingshead. Philadelphia, 1984.